$\mathcal{W}$rapped in $\mathcal{C}$olor:
Stranded Knitting in the 21st Century

Dedication

To Elizabeth Stockwell Dunkell Branham, *a.k.a* Gramma, who gave me that all-important unconditional parental love and approval. Gramma not only stirred my love for knitting, but also she made me believe all those early, wonky, trapezoidal hole-filled scarves I knitted were perfect. I think about you every day, Gramma.

Table of Contents

Acknowledgments

I am a technidiot, and I could not have completed this project without the tireless help of so many of my knitting friends. Andrew, my husband, is not a knitter, but he has endured my whining over my knitting and writing capabilities—as well as the longer list of my incapabilities—for long months. He'd rather be watching TV. Thank you, Andrew. To the longsuffering members of my Ravelry group and to those I have burdened with endless email questions, I thank you for your patience and kind responses. To all the beautiful women who agreed to model my designs, Pia, Alyssa, Stacey, Solange and the "Cow Gals," at The Black Cow in Croton, thanks so much. To my wonderful knitting pals in my local knitting group, Croton on Hudson Gab and Knit, your support is priceless. I'd be lost without you. To Meaghan for coming up with the title I love—it's perfect. To Petra for taking great photos of the design pieces, you made Wrapped explode with color. Thank you Wendy Preston for introducing me to the fantastic world of colorwork. It has changed my life. Who knew? To Wendy and Jeanette Gingold please know how much I appreciate your support, practical help, and your endless willingness to share your vast publishing knowledge with me. A very special and heartfelt thank you to Marjorie Anderson, who undertook my every question as a doctoral thesis, doing all kinds of research to answer me accurately and thoroughly each and every time. I am so lucky to have so many wise, talented and kind women as friends. In a very real way, you are my family.

Preface

So many knitters—even seasoned ones—see colorwork as something complex and beyond their abilities. Not so very long ago, I was quite intimidated by the idea of stranding, and books that I looked at on the technique did not allay my fears. I want to show all knitters that stranded knitting is far easier than they might think, and that very complicated-looking designs are simple to knit. My illustrations and easy-to-follow explanations will give even the most hesitant knitters the confidence to create beautiful garments and accessories. By using the knit stitch alone—because I design in the round, my patterns for the most part do not require purling—even the most inexperienced knitters can create pieces that comprise intricate colowork ideas. Stranded knitting is deceptively easy.

Wrapped in Color offers a fresh and welcome approach to stranded knitting. It is a total departure from traditional stranding style. With a choice collection of my new-fashioned colorwork-in-the-round patterns, accompanied by many attractive photos, there is something in this book that will appeal to young knitters, as well as those who are young at heart. I have replaced the traditional ideas of what colorwork is with new designs that have never been done before. While any text included will be informative, it will be light, interesting, casual and entertaining.

The book is long on visuals, tutorials and charts and short on written text. It covers all that color can accomplish in a knitted piece. Color can convey mood. Color can be lace. Color can be cables. Color can be texture. In short, color can be anything, and anyone can knit it.

Introduction

Many Fair Isle books open with the history of Fair Isle and other stranded knitting techniques. Too many books do that. If you are like me, you skip over those pages to get to the good stuff. I will spare you that history lesson but, because books need some text, I will supply a more personal history for those who don't want to jump right to the yummy patterns.

When I was growing up, I liked nothing better than to curl up and lose myself in a good Nancy Drew mystery. Well, maybe I liked chocolate cake better, but that doesn't work in this part of the story. For all of my reading life, I have been able to completely lose my sense of time and work-a-day reality when immersed in a great read. I couldn't imagine anything better. Until I learned stranded knitting. I have been knitting since I was five years old, but my foray into the world of colorwork is relatively recent. Like so many seasoned knitters, colorwork seemed daunting and far beyond my abilities.

When Wendy Preston first joined our local knitting group, she brought in some of her lovely projects to show us. One of them was her *Mardi Gras* sweater (by Alice Starmore), and I was slack-jawed-blown-away. "You *knit* that? How did you *do* that?!" She told me it was Fair Isle and, honestly, I had never heard of the technique. I had seen sweaters worked in it, but I assumed they were knitted on machines. I had been knitting for 45 years, and I had never come across "Fair Isle," or my memory failed me on that one. Nevertheless,

I was blown away, and I knew I had to learn this technique. So, I bought two balls of contrasting wool, a couple of how-to books, and I practiced. Ever compliant, I did just as the instructions demanded. I held one yarn in my right hand and one in my left. But try as I might, I could not achieve even tensions between the two. I am a thrower. My left hand is useless except for holding a needle or getting coffee and the afore-mentioned chocolate cake to my mouth (and, make no mistake, coffee and chocolate are as important to knitting as wool). So, I kept practicing, but now, I simply knitted with one yarn in my right hand, dropped it and picked up the other strand as I needed it. This worked, but it was clumsy and slow-going. I needed something more convenient. Enter: toes. I put the second (sometimes called background) yarn between my toes and sat back. It worked like a charm. I threw the first (foreground strand) yarn with my right hand as usual and then, when I needed to knit a stitch with the other strand, I just hooked it with my pinky, or any other convenient digit, and kept going. A revised version of this bizarre method still works for me today. Now, I thread both yarns in my toes, much as I thread my sewing machine, and zip right along changing colors as my chart dictates. When knitting colorwork patterns, I lose all sense of reality as we usually know it in our waking hours. It is pure zen for me—the pure, in-the-moment, meditative existence that is bliss. Honestly, I am so very lucky to be able to spend my days doing what I love to do. And the only way I can increase my joy is to show others how to achieve knitting nirvana, too.

What is Colorwork?

Colorwork is a generic term applied to knitting that employs more than one color yarn. Even simply striped pieces can be called colorwork, for example. Several techniques can be worked to achieve colorwork. We'll discuss three of the more commonly used methods here: *intarsia, slip- stitch colorwork* and, the method used in creating all of the patterns in this book, *stranded.*

Intarsia is a technique wherein fields of different colors, which seem to be inlaid in one another, are merely separate pieces worked together as you go like pieces of a jigsaw puzzle. Unlike alternative colorwork techniques, intarsia employs the use of only one active color at a time. The unused strands of yarn are not carried across the back but are left dangling while the current color is worked. Rather than worked in the round as with other colorwork techniques, intarsia is commonly worked flat, or back and forth.

If, for example, the knitter is creating a blue square on a white background (See Fig. A), she will knit across the background with white yarn until she reaches the part that requires blue for the square. She will then drop the white yarn, attach or pick up the blue, knit the width of the square, then drop the blue strand and pick up or attach a white strand and continue across. For the next row, she will turn the work around, purl back across the background with the white yarn, drop it and pick up blue for her square, purl the square, drop that strand, pick up the white strand she had dropped on the previous row and continue across purling the background white. This method works well for objects that require large areas of solid colors. However, it can become difficult if the design has several different blocks of color (See Fig. B). You can imagine the possible tangles, working with small yarn bundles of many different colors dangling along your work.

Fig. A   (front and back)

Fig. B

Intarsia pillow courtesy of Wendy Preston

The slip-stitch colorwork technique creates a color design by carrying colored stitches up from a previously knitted row. (See Fig. C) The basic slip stitch is created when the stitch is passed from the left needle to the right needle without being knitted. It can be slipped with the yarn held in the back or in the front to achieve various effects. If the slipped stitch is knitted on the next row, the slipped stitch will, naturally, be twice as tall as its neighboring stitches. (See Fig. D) Knitting in this manner over many rows creates a vertical column of these doubly tall stitches forming a pleasing colorwork design, especially when worked in a contrasting color or colors. The slip-stitch colorwork technique lends itself particularly well to a variety of designs, especially mosaic and geometric patterns, or designs with rounded edges. (See Fig. E) The slip-stitch stranding method does have limitations relative to other colorwork techniques, however. It can lack drape and be stiff and dense due to all of the slipped stitches.

Fig. C   **Fig. D**   **Fig E.**

Stranded knitting is, by far, my colorwork method of choice. The design possibilities are virtually endless. And, because it can be accomplished almost exclusively in-the-round (as opposed to flat, or back and forth), I can almost completely avoid purling, my personal *bête noir*.

This is not to say you can't strand back and forth; you can. But, you don't have to. A colorwork chart can be read to accommodate either flat or in-the-round knitting. I will explain how to read charts both ways later on. Most of us have referred to the stranded method as Fair Isle, but there is a slight distinction. Fair Isle (and here comes that history I promised not to include) is named after designs emanating from an Island by that name, which is north of Scotland and is one of the Shetland Islands. But while Fair Isle only uses two strands of yarn in a given round and has a limited palette of very few colors, stranded rounds in general can comprise two, three or even four color strands per round, and the color possibilities are only as limited as the knitter's imagination. In short, while all Fair Isle is stranded, not all stranded is Fair Isle. (See Figs. F and G)

Fig. F (Fair Isle) front   back   Fig. G (Stranded)

In-the-round knitting is my preferred colorwork technique. The piece, even if it will eventually be a flat object, is knitted on a circular needle. Knitting this way results in stockinette, which is the perfect stitch for showing off colorwork design, (See Fig. H) while simultaneously avoiding that pesky, every-other-row purling. Because the knitter works continuously, around and around on a circular needle, "rows" are referred to, obviously enough, as "rounds." A sweater constructed in the round can be worked almost entirely as one piece, with very little, if any, seaming involved. Even cardigans can be knitted in the round by employing steeks, a technique I will explain shortly.

Fig. H

The stockinette stitch creates columns of those lovely little "V" shapes. It can be achieved either by working in the round, working the knit stitch only, or back and forth necessitating purling every other row.

Knitting flat means exactly what it sounds like. Using straight needles, the piece is worked back and forth by alternating knit and purl rows. The final object, if it is a sweater for example, is constructed by sewing or grafting the flat pieces together.

Traditionally, rules have existed for the "proper" way to hold yarns while stranding. We have the *Portuguese* method, the *Continental* method and the practice of holding both yarns in one hand, called *One-hand* stranding.

The Portuguese method of yarn-holding uses other body parts in addition to the hands. (I like the idea!) It is an old method, but it is not as commonly used in North America as in other parts of the world. The knitter holds her yarns around her neck, and the yarn is sometimes placed in a pin on her lapel. This practice frees up her hands, gives relief to that poor index finger used for tensioning in Continental knitting, and yarn tension issues are taken care of almost unconsciously. (See Fig. I) The technique also helps prevent the yarns from tangling.

Fig. I

When stranding Continental style, the knitter holds her dominant yarn in one hand and her background yarn in the other. She scoops the yarn she wants for a given stitch, as needed. (See Fig. J) I learned this way, and technically I could do it, but I was unable to achieve equal tension between the two hands, even after much practice. Perhaps this was so because I am a "thrower" rather than a "picker." Perhaps you have avoided colorwork for the same reason. No need to be afraid any longer. No more rules!

Fig. J

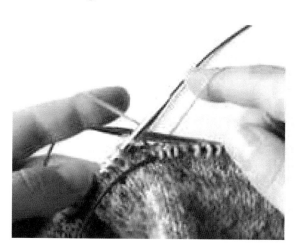

Some of us are "throwers." That is to say, we pick up our yarn with our right hand (if we are right-handed) and wrap it around the left needle to form a stitch rather than just scoop the yarn from our left index finger with the right-hand needle, which is what "pickers" do. Like the Portuguese-method knitters, I need more body parts than just my hands, Unlike the Portuguese-method knitters, I don't use my neck. I use my feet! We need to name this style, I guess. Generically, using one hand has been called, obviously enough, one-handed stranding. Some knitters merely pick up the yarn they need for a stitch, throw, drop it when they need to switch colors, and pick up the other color and throw.

If we use our toes, and "we" do, maybe we should call it toe-handed knitting. (See Fig. K) As with Portuguese knitting, the use of my toes frees up my fingers and keeps the tension even. And the method keeps the yarns from tangling.

Fig. K

As I stated above, there are no hard and fast rules for holding your yarn. Don't be put off if you can't get the knack of a particular colorwork method. Do what works for you. If you can accomplish a piece that looks as nice on the back as it does on the front, you are doing it correctly. You will find a method that works for you. Most important is to find a way that makes stranding a joy.

Who can Knit Colorwork?

You can! If you can make a knit stitch, you can do colorwork. It is easier than you think. Really, it is! The only difference between knitting and colorwork is that you alternate between color strands in colorwork. Generally, you are working with two strands at a time. First one and then the other per specific pattern instructions. It is simply a matter of grabbing the strand color needed for a particular stitch.

It is my strong assertion that, in the past, knitters have over-complicated the colorwork process, scaring away prospective stranders. By adhering strictly to a "right" way of accomplishing it, stranders have made colorwork seem more like rocket science than simply knitting with two colors at once. To those I say, "technique-schmechnique!" As I stated earlier, some have success holding one strand in each hand. Others wrap strands around their neck. Some use one hand for both yarns. I use my toes. Look, if it works for you, it's the right way. As long as your tension is not overly tight, which causes puckering, or overly loose and your floats are even and frequent, you are knitting your project correctly.

If you have been put off by tutorials telling you that you must hold your yarn a certain way in order to achieve great-looking colorwork, be put- off no more! Old, stuffy rules are history. I am living proof that you can hold your yarns any way that feels comfortable and works for you. As you've seen, I use my toes. This practice happened accidentally, but it serves me well. And it keeps the yarns separated, lightly tensioned and easy to grab. Requirements? Clean feet and an impeccable pedicure. Toes may or may not work for you. You will find your own way to easily hold both strands, keep them from twisting and keep the tension even.

Why would a knitter want to knit with color, anyway? What can color accomplish? Color can, all by itself, create a variety of knitting styles without the knitter having to make lots of complicated stitches to get there. For me, it can accomplish looks I love but don't really enjoy knitting, like lace with those pesky yarn overs and purls, and cables with those pesky, well, cables. I love the look of cables, but I am not a fan of the concentration and work required to achieve them. With colorwork, I can just let myself go and knit. Lazy, you say? Perhaps, but blissfully so! Plus, the fabric created by working the cables for real tends to be bulky and lack drape, whereas colorwork cables are no more dense than a stranded stockinette piece. The fabric is more pliable and can have drape. Goodness knows, I love drape.

In short, color can be anything you want it to be. Color can be lace, cables, double-knit, texture, sunscreen, even love. I will prove it to you. Below are some patterns I designed to create these looks through the use of color alone. No fuss. No muss!

Choosing Your Pattern

First and foremost, you want to choose a pattern you will enjoy working. It is not fun to force yourself to do something you don't like even before it's finished. Knitting is a joy. The process should be as much fun as realizing the finished product. Find something you like, and you can knit it. Do you enjoy knitting hats? Does a shawl appeal to you? Are you interested in a short-term project? (That's me, by the way. I am fond of saying that my attention span is about a hat long.) If you like a particular project, but you think it will be too difficult, fear not. It is no more challenging than a hat, a scarf or mitts, I promise you. All are equally easy to work.

If you are new to colorwork, you might want to take design complexity into consideration for the first project. Once you get the hang of reading colorwork charts, changing colors, working even tension, you will be able to work even the most intricate designs. Some knitters have practiced working a couple swatches and felt comfortable enough to start in with a detailed colorwork pattern. If you feel more comfortable starting more slowly, I recommend a two-color design, or one with fewer color changes. This will allow you to see fast progress, quick results, and will give you the confidence you need to work a more complicated design. And I use the word "complicated" loosely here because no pattern is really all that difficult.

Choosing Your Yarn

An important feature of colorwork is the pattern design itself. If you want to highlight the colorwork design, you will want to use a hardtwist yarn. A hardtwist fiber will produce great stitch definition and will highlight the design the pattern intends. Hardtwist is a yarn that lacks a halo, those furry, hairy little fibers that stick out and make the yarn appear fuzzy. Although very soft and appealing, yarns like this tend to obscure the stitch pattern. On the other hand, if you want to blur or soften the design, a haloed yarn might be a choice you prefer. The edges of one color will blend with the next color, creating an effect different from, but not necessarily less appealing than, the same design worked with a hardtwist. You are the artist. The choice is yours.

Although colorwork can be worked with any weight yarn, (lace, fingering, DK, worsted, and so on), it is good to keep in mind that, when stranding, you will automatically add thickness and bulk to your piece by virtue of the fact that you are carrying the unused yarn across the back of your work. If you choose to use a heavier yarn, and you still want drape, be sure to increase the needle size. If you want a stiffer, denser fabric, use a smaller needle for a more tightly knit project.

My colorwork yarn weight of choice is fingering, and I prefer wool over cotton or acrylic. Wool works up easily, blocks better, and generally keeps its shape better than other yarns. For hats and fingering-weight wool, a #3 needle works well. For my shawls, because I want to produce a loose, fabric with lots of drape, I will use a #9 needle. Again, you are the artist, and you make the choice for your project. Work some swatches until you get the look and feel you want. Just make sure you adjust gauge so the size remains true.

Photo of "Isadora," courtesy of Miss Babs

Choosing Your Colors

OK. You have your pattern and you know what you want to accomplish with your yarn choice and needle size. What about color? Color is a key ingredient, of course. This is colorwork after all. The same pattern, worked up in one color scheme will change its total appearance and give off a completely different vibe when worked up in an alternate color scheme. Are you looking to create a cool, wintery feel? Choose blues, aquas, and whites. Do you want a warm glow of autumn to shine through? Use autumnal colors. If it's a boy: baby blue. If it's a girl: pink. That was written sarcastically. I am old. You use whatever colors you want for baby! Anything goes. It's your project and the world of color is your palette. You can buy literally any shade in yarn these days. What a great time to knit with color!

Top: courtesy of Aimee on Ravelry Bottom: courtesy of Anneism on Ravelry

Tension and Floats

Achieving an even, consistent tension takes practice. And that's all it takes. You will want to find a way to hold your yarn, get comfortable with it and then concentrate on carrying your yarns and working the stitches in a way that creates a smooth, nearly-flat fabric. The piece won't be completely smooth until after soaking and blocking. The finishing process relaxes the yarn and evens out tiny "bumps." However, if you pull your carried yarns too tightly across the back (called floating) the work will pucker and no amount of blocking will solve the problem completely. When floating your unused strand across the back of your work remember LEO. Float LOOSELY, EVENLY and OFTEN. Remember, the backs of your projects should always look as nice and neat as the front. Please take a few minutes to review my YouTube tutorial on tension and floats here:

http://www.youtube.com/watch?v=jQlc4UQWuzc

Yarn Dominance

The above video leads us to the related issue of yarn dominance, a thing I described in the tutorial without specifically naming it. Yarn dominance refers to the way you carry your yarn to produce a dominant color on the front. You noticed in my baby sweater that most of the time, I held the white yarn in the dominant, or "over" position, crossing it over the pink on the back when necessary. But, for that one knitting period, I inadvertently switched my yarns, making the pink the yarn carried in the "over" position. This changed the appearance on the front, creating an unwanted pinkish stripe in the fabric. You will want to pay attention to yarn dominance. Some designs show inconsistencies more than others, but as long as you hold the yarns in the same position each time you knit, you will avoid trouble. If you hold color A in your right hand and color B in your left...always hold them in those hands. If you get up to make a cup of coffee and come back and pick the yarns up the other way (A in your left hand and B in your right), you will have that disturbing color variation on the front. If color A is between your big toe and second toe, and color B is held by your pinky toe, keep the yarns in those toe positions throughout the project.

Lucy Neatby's Paradoxical Mittens Courtesy of Wendy Preston

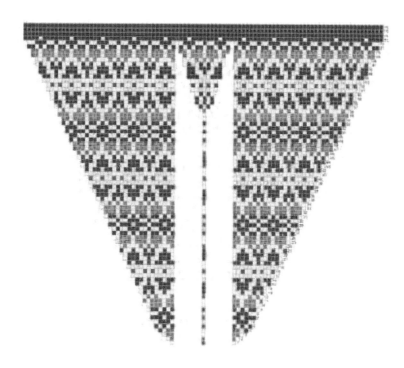

Reading Colorwork Charts

Reading colorwork charts is much the same as reading other knitting charts. But there are differences. We'll discuss similarities first. Like most charts, colorwork charts are generally read from right to left and from bottom to top. If you are working rows back and forth, the purl rows will be numbered on the left, and you work them from left to right. In short, you start working on the side of the chart where you see the row number, and you work across from that point. Each square of the chart grid represents one stitch.

Like lace charts, decreases and future increases on colorwork charts are denoted by blank spaces, showing the lack of stitch where one used to be or where one will be, eventually.

Now for the major difference: Lacework chart squares are filled with symbols representing the type of stitch to be worked in that spot, and they are accompanied by legends that explain what the symbols mean. Colorwork charts are written differently. Because colorwork in the round is worked all in stockinette, the knit stitch is a given. There is no need to mark the stitch type, except occasionally when a purl stitch is required. The grid and or instructions will give directions. What the knitter does need to know is which color to work in a particular spot. So, colorwork charts have colors in the squares, rather than symbols, and color key legends where needed to describe what color stitches to make and where.

See Youtube tutorial here:
http://www.youtube.com/watch?v=rMyZXIsxF
hw

Courtesy of Thiagram on Ravelry

Steeks

Steeks are additional waste stitches (usually 10 to 12) added to a piece that allow the knitter to keep working in the round. (See Sample chart on next page.) The steek stitches will be cut after the knitting is completed, allowing the piece to open up or lie flat. Steeks are the perfect innovation for knitters, like me, who don't want to purl or read a colorwork chart "backward." Steeks allow you to knit the entire body of a sweater in one tubular piece, even if it will eventually be a cardigan. After the body of the piece is constructed, the steek stitches are cut (See photo above), and then they are tacked down to form a hem or facing. Armholes can be steeked so sleeves can be added later. Are you horrified at the thought of cutting into your work? I heard a real horror story of a knitter who worked an entire colorwork sweater and then, when cutting her steek, cut through both layers of her sweater, completely ruining it. That's really terrible, but it isn't life or death, and it's about the worst thing that could happen.

Lesson vicariously learned! If you are careful to separate your front and back (by placing the tube over an ironing board end, for example), you will eliminate the risk of cutting through both layers of your piece. Once you try steeking, you will see the advantages of wasting a few extra knitted stitches over working a piece flat and trying to keep track of the pattern on purl rows. My *Saxony* pattern appears in the chapter Color as Shape on page 48. This five-sided capelet employs steeks. What a perfect time to try out the technique. I bet you fall in love with it!

Sample Steek Chart

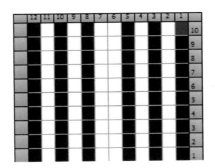

Color as Lace

First, let's consider how color can achieve a lacy, drapey look by employing the knit stitch only. You can knit lace with color alone. No purls. No yarn overs. By designing patterns with lots of subtle swirls and either highly-contrasting colors or only slight shade differences, I have accomplished a lacy look that is deceptively easy to knit. The first pattern is *Smoke and Mirrors*, an elegant shawl that can be worn for evening dress or, more casually, with jeans. It is versatile and, while I chose a sparkly hard-twist black Merino for the background and a misty gray fingering wool for the smoke, the color choice is up to the knitter. I can see this in lovely aquas and blues, looking fresh and watery. I can see it in starkly contrasting colors to create a more dramatic look. The shawl is large and full of drape. It can be worn any number of ways, depending on the wearer's mood.

When stranding, you are working with twice as much wool because you carry the unused strand along the back as you knit with the other strand. This can hamper a nice, loose, drape. To return drape to the desired lace-like garment, simply increase the needle size. I work with fingering-weight wools as I strand, but to achieve great drape, I use a #9 or even a #10 needle.

Smoke and Mirrors Stranded Shawl©

by Deborah Tomasello

Courtesy of Gabby Jacobson

Size: TBD by Knitter (at least 48" diameter)

Materials: 200 g (approx 900 yards) of fingering-weight black sparkles yarn (Cover shawl used Galloping Jester's *Midnight*)
150 g (approx. 700 yds) of fingering-weight very light gray yarn (Cover shawl used KnitPicks Palette *Mist*)
**Any fingering-weight yarn will do
One multi-length cable #9 circular needle, five #9 DPNs, Stitch markers, and tapestry needle

Abbreviations: M1 = Make a st in st just knitted see video:
http://www.youtube.com/watch?v=NW7Un1gXRmc
PM = Place marker.

Instructions: Using 2 DPNs, CO 3 sts using *Midnight*.
K1 row.
Purl back for 2nd row.
K1, M1 for 6 sts total.

Purl 6 sts.
K1, M1 across 12 sts total.
Purl 12 sts.
K1, (K1, M1) for 18 sts
total. Purl 18 sts.
K2 (K1, M1) for 24 sts total.

Split sts evenly on 3 DPNs, 8 sts on each needle, placing markers every four sts. Begin following chart here. Continue to work in the round. (You will sew opening closed later.)

IMPORTANT: Float evenly and loosely every two stitches for a neat- looking shawl back.

Work CHART A as follows: PM, K one chart repeat, PM around (6 chart repeats per round. 6 markers placed.) When you have increased enough sts to warrant it, move work from DPNs to short circular, and switch to longer cable lengths as needed throughout.

After completing round 75, detach *Mist*. With *Midnight*, knit the next three rounds. BO loosely.

Finishing: With tail from CO, sew closed small slit left at the beginning when knitting the first few rounds. Tie and weave in or trim all color change ends. Wash and block flat.

On reading the chart: Please see my YouTube video that explains how to read my colorwork charts and how/where do make the increases: http://www.youtube.com/watch?v=NW7Un1gXRmc

The work on the back should look as nice as the work on the front:

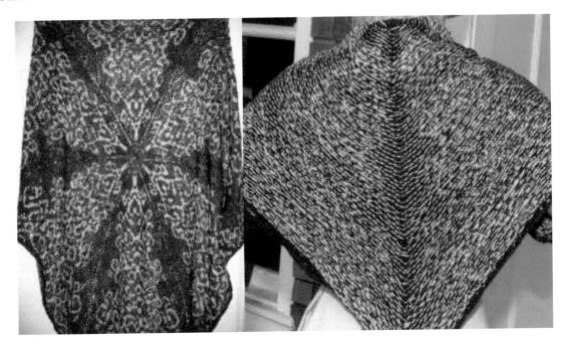

CHART A

(Next page)

Perhaps you'd like to start with a smaller "lace" project. *The Hermitage: The Mitts* was inspired by a picture I saw of a room in the world-famous Hermitage Museum in St Petersburg, Russia. When I saw pictures of those beautiful light blue walls accented by other blues and ornamented with gold accents, I knew I had to design from it. (See Fig. L.) The room looks like lace. It bespeaks a stately elegance. Adding gold beads to the mitts helps recreate the beauty of the room.

Fig. L

I have designed some cool features into this mitt, too. So that you can keep on texting, I made the top cuff long enough to fold down over a secret pocket that can hold valuables and free up fingers. If you want your fingers covered, you can unfold the cuff and pull the drawstring closed to form a cozy mitten. Either way, because they're stranded, these mitts have double the wool and double the cozy warmth. This lacy beauty is achieved through color. Only the ribbing calls for some fancy-schmancy purling.

The HERMITAGE Mittens and KEEP on TEXTIN' Fingerless Gloves©

by Deborah Tomasello

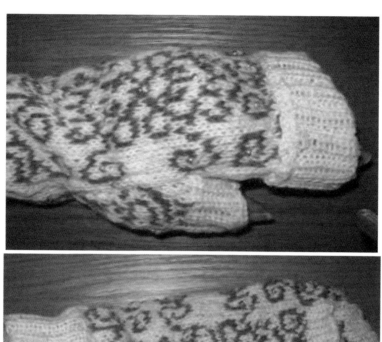

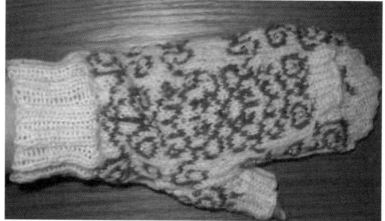

Size: Woman's Medium

Materials: 1 ball each of KnitPicks Palette: *Clarity* and *Brass Heather*

#3 circular needle or five #3 DPNs (or size needed to obtain gauge)

**Any fingering-weight yarn will do

tapestry needle

6mm beads, if desired, and a small crochet hook for attaching them

Gauge: 32 stitches and 32 rounds = 4" using #3 needles

Abbreviations: K2TOG = Knit two stitches together.

SSK = Slip one stitch, then slip the next. Insert left needle into the front loops of the slipped stitches and knit them together from this position.

MITTS:

Pocket: CO 20 stitches with *Clarity*. Knit, in stockinette, about 30 rows or 3.5 inches. End with a purl row. DO NOT Bind off. Steam block. Set aside.

Mitt: With DPNs, CO 56 sts (14 sts on each of 4 DPNs) using *Caribbean*. Knit 2x2 rib for 16 rounds.

Knitting first round: Inc 8 sts (Inc 2 sts evenly on each of 4 needles). Knit 64 sts according to CHART A through round 13. (**See tutorial for bead placement here**) Continue to follow chart, and inc for thumb as follows:

Thumb Increase Round 14: m1, k1, m1 in first st (3 sts now in first st). Continue to k sts as shown around
Round 15: knit all sts according to chart
Round 16: m1, k3, m1, cont. to k sts around as shown
Round 17: knit all sts around according to chart
Round 18: m1, k5, m1, cont. to k sts around as shown
Round 19: knit all sts around according to chart
Round 20: m1, k7, m1, cont. to k sts around as shown
Round 21: knit all sts around according to chart
Round 22: m1, k9, m1, cont. to k sts around as shown
Round 23: knit all sts around according to chart
Round 24: m1, k11, m1, cont. to k sts around as shown
Round 25: knit all sts around according to chart
Round 26: m1, k13, m1, cont. to k sts around as shown
Round 27: knit all sts around according to chart
Round 28: m1, k15, m1, cont. to k sts around as shown
Round 29: knit all sts around according to chart
Round 30: m1, k17, m1 cont. to k sts around as shown

Round 31: knit all sts around according to chart
Round 32: m1, k19, m1 cont. to k sts around as shown
Round 33: knit all sts around according to chart

Round 34: Move 21 thumb sts to fifth DPN (or waste yarn) to be worked as thumb later. M1 st in next st so you will be working the chart's 64 sts. Follow chart around with 64 stitches on needles.

Rounds 35 to 48: Knit chart.

Pocket: Round 49: Add pocket—Knit 6 stitches. Move next 20 sts to stitch holder. Retrieve needle with pocket stitches, and with pocket front (stockinette side) facing you, continue to knit chart with these stitches.

Knit chart through round 58.

Knit 2x2 rib using *Clarity* for 20 rounds (2.5 inches to completely cover fingers or fold back when you want fingers exposed).
Bind off loosely.

Move 20 stitches from stitch holder to needle. Attach *Clarity* and knit 2x2 rib for 6 rows. Bind off. Sew rib sides to mitt, creating the pocket top.

Thumb:

Using *Clarity*, pick up 7 sts from body of mitten, knit 21sts on 5th DPN (split so you're working on 3 needles) for a total of 28 thumb sts. Join. Knit 2x2 rib for 16 rounds in *Clarity*. (Or 2" to completely cover thumb, and fold back when you want thumb exposed!) Bind off.

Finishing: Crochet chain long enough to fit top circumference of mitt rib. Leave tails long enough to attach and tie. With tapestry needle, weave chain, loosely, through each rib at the top of mitt. Tie chain ends SECURLY in the back, weave in and trim ends. Now, when chain loop is gently tugged from other side, the mitt top will close up, creating a warm mitten. (See cover photo.) Stitch pocket to mitt from the inside.

Fold top cuff over pocket cuff to secure valuables. Tie and trim all yarn ends. Wash and block.

CHART A

Yellow squares note places where beads are added.

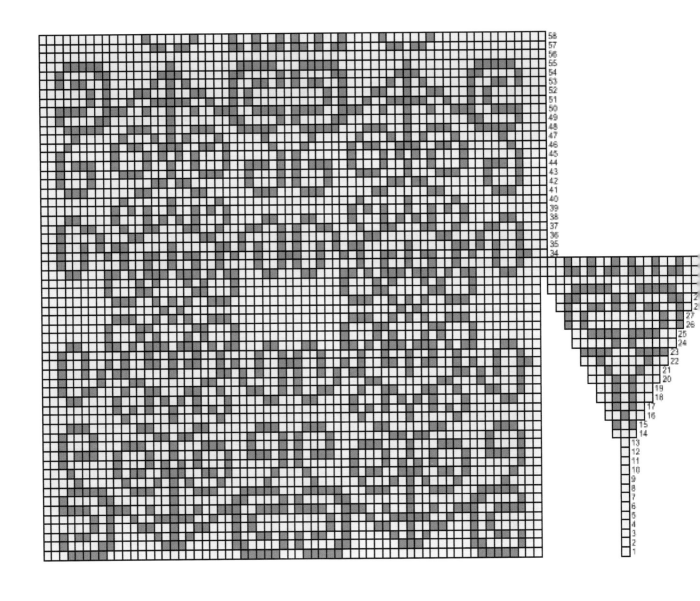

Color as Doubleknit

Double-knitting is a technique that creates a two-sided stockinette-stitch object, with one side being the color reverse of the other. Generally, the knitter reads the chart and, using the opposing color and purling every other stitch, knits both sides at once. I have attempted this. The look is beautiful. But, I am a lazy knitter. I am always looking for an easier way to get the results I want. How did I make "double-knitting" easier? Again, the answer is color!

To further show you the versatility of colorwork, I designed a cowl pattern that simulates double-knitting without the concentration and work required to accomplish it. People will think you're a genius, and all you did was knit around and around. No sweat and no cursing. Just pure joy.

The *Wowl Cowl* scratches so many knitting itches! It is worked in the round, is reversible, and it employs an easy-to-follow colorwork design comprising only the knit stitch. It can be knitted any length. It can be a cowl, a moebius cowl or a scarf. EZ-PZ!

Faux Double-Knit Wowl Cowl©

by Deborah Tomasello

Sizes: One size fits all

Materials: One 100 g skein each of any two Lisa Souza TIMARU contrasting or coordinating colors (Cover cowl uses Mulberry and Blimey.)

One 16" circular #3 needle, stitch markers, and tapestry needle

Gauge: 32 stitches and 32 rounds = 4" using #3 needles, but gauge is unimportant here.

FOR COWL: Using scrap yarn of contrasting color or a provisional CO, CO 96 st, placing one marker at the round beginning and one after the 48th st (1/2 way). Join to beginning being careful not to twist sts. Knit three rounds. Detach scrap yarn and add working yarns to begin CHART A.

FOR SCARF: Using either color, CO 96 st, placing marker at round beginning and another after 48th st (1/2 way).

NOTE: Breaking my floating rules here, you will be carrying yarn across 6 sts without floating. Normally I would float them, but because the back will be completely hidden, do not float across the 6 st on most rounds. Only float every 5-6 sts on the solid color rounds.

Work CHART A beginning with round 1. Work as many 16-round pattern repeats as you want until you reach the desired length, ending with round 8 for the scarf and round 16 for the cowl.

For scarf, BO. For cowl, pick up live sts of main color at beginning (then remove scrap yarn), graft to those live sts—add one twist before grafting for a moebius cowl.

Finishing: Tie and trim all yarn ends. Damp block with steam iron and damp cloth so that the piece is blocked in half, each half being the reverse of the other. Make sure edges are straight and crisp. For scarf, make and tie fringes on each end.

CHART A

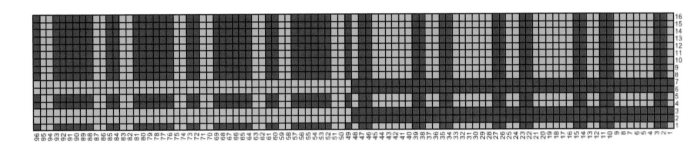

Color as Cables

I love the look of knitted cables. I have admired the classic cabled sweaters, the newer cables shawl designs, and the wonderfully complex Celtic cabled projects. I know how to work cables. I just don't enjoy making them the standard way. My solution? Color, of course! Color as cables? Who'da thunk it? But it is easily doable. No cable needle required. With only one light shade of color for the cable and somewhat darker shade of the same color for the background shadowing cables naturally form, you can create cables with color alone. No purling. Just knitting. Color can do anything! Following is a colorwork cabled hat pattern I designed to show you the possibilities. Using this technique, you can knit lazy cable sweaters, socks, or almost anything else. You can even raise the cable, if you'd like, by working a garter stitch in the cable portion of the design. I don't do that, though because, you guessed it, I'd have to purl!

Crazy Lazy Cables HAT©

by *Deborah Tomasello*

Courtesy of Orit

Size: Adult and Teen 21"- 23"

Materials: 50 g each of KnitPicks Palette or any fingering-weight wool:
Cover: *Mai Tai Heather* and *Kumquat Heather*
Or choose a light and a dark shade of any one color
**Any fingering-weight yarn will do
One 16" #3 circular needle, four #3 DPNs (or size needed to obtain gauge), stitch marker, and tapestry needle

Gauge: 32 stitches and 32 rounds = 4" using #3 needles

Abbreviations: K2TOG = Knit two stitches together.
SSK = Slip one stitch, then slip the next. Insert left needle into the front loops of the slipped stitches and knit them together from this position.

Instructions: With circular needle, CO 136 sts using *Kumquat Heather (or darker shade)*. Join to work in round, placing stitch marker and being careful not to twist stitches. Knit six rounds corrugated rib (see CHART A) using *lighter shade* for knit sts and *darker shade* for purl sts.

Increase round: Using *darker shade*, inc evenly to 168 sts (knit 4, {knit 4 make 1 around to last 4 stitches} knit last 4 stitches).

Follow CHART B (6 repeats per round) for 69 rounds, decreasing as indicated and switching to DPNs when necessary. (Each dec round has 2 decreases next to each other; k2tog for first dec, and ssk for second each time.) After round 69, with 12 sts. on the needles, k2tog around. 6 sts remain. Knit last six sts for 5 rounds; cut yarn leaving a tail several inches long. Move all sts from needles to tapestry needle, and pull tightly. Secure from the inside.

Finishing: Tie and weave in or trim all color change ends. Wash and block to fit.

CHART A

Use *lighter shade* for knit sts and *darker shade* for purl sts.

Dash in st means purl.

	4	3	2	1	
	—	—			6
	—	—			5
	—	—			4
	—	—			3
	—	—			2
	—	—			1

CHART B

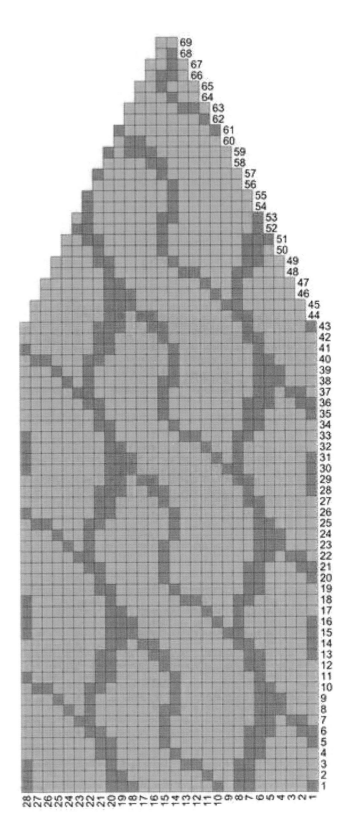

Color as Texture

Texture is an element of knitting that can create interest or attention focus to an area of the piece. The garter stitch alone is full of texture with its little bumps and ridges. Ribbing, a combination of knit and purl stitches yielding a classic, stretchy textured feature in many knitting patterns. By combining the knit and purl stitch in a different way, the knitter can make a basket-weave fabric. (See Fig. M.) Beads also add texture.

It won't surprise you to learn that colorwork can create texture, too. Notice the ribbing-like effect in the featured design below (*Ginko Leaf Cowl*). There is no ribbing here, just the illusion of ribbing created by the way the strands are carried and floated across the back. In order to achieve ribs, I have floated every 2nd stitch. If you alternate the floats in your own arrangement, say, every 2nd st on even sts on even rounds, and every 2nd stitch on odd st numbers on odd rounds, you'll achieve a unique and interesting textured look all your own. Possible floating arrangements are endless. Change up the way you carry and float, and create a different textured effect.

Fig. M

Ginko Textured Two-Sided Cowl©

by Deborah Tomasello

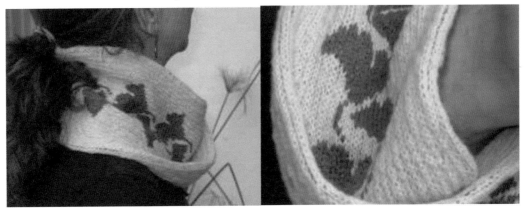

Courtesy of Solange LaBonne

Courtesy of Hannah

Sizes: One size fits all

Materials: Two 50 g balls each of KnitPicks Palette: *Oyster Heather*
and *Clover* (or more for a longer cowl)
**Any fingering-weight yarn will do
One 16" circular #3 needle
Stitch markers and tapestry needle

Gauge: 32 stitches and 32 rounds = 4" using #3 needles, but gauge is unimportant here

FOR COWL: Using scrap yarn of contrasting color or a provisional CO, CO 120 st, placing one marker at the round beginning and one after the 60th st (1/2 way). Join to beginning being careful not to twist sts. Knit 2 or 3 rounds. Detach scrap yarn and add working yarns to begin Chart A.

NOTE: The texture in this project is created entirely by the floats. In order to achieve the ribbing effect shown in the cover photo, float every second stitch and in the exact same places throughout, regardless of yarn color used. If you would prefer a mottled texture, float on the even stitch numbers on even rounds and odd stitch numbers on the odd-numbered rounds. Or mix things up and create your own variation of texture.

Work Chart A beginning with round 1. Work as many 21-round repeats as you want until you reach the desired length, ending with round 21.

Pick up live stitches at beginning (then remove scrap yarn), graft to those live sts-- add one twist before grafting for a moebius cowl, or leave untwisted for a regular cowl. Make longer if you want to be able to double the cowl around the neck.

Finishing: Tie and trim all yarn ends. Soak and block dry so that the piece is blocked in half, each half being the centered the same as the other. Make sure edges are straight and crisp.

CHART A (I have repeated round 1 on top for easier reference when repeating chart. Chart here contains four 21-round repeats.)

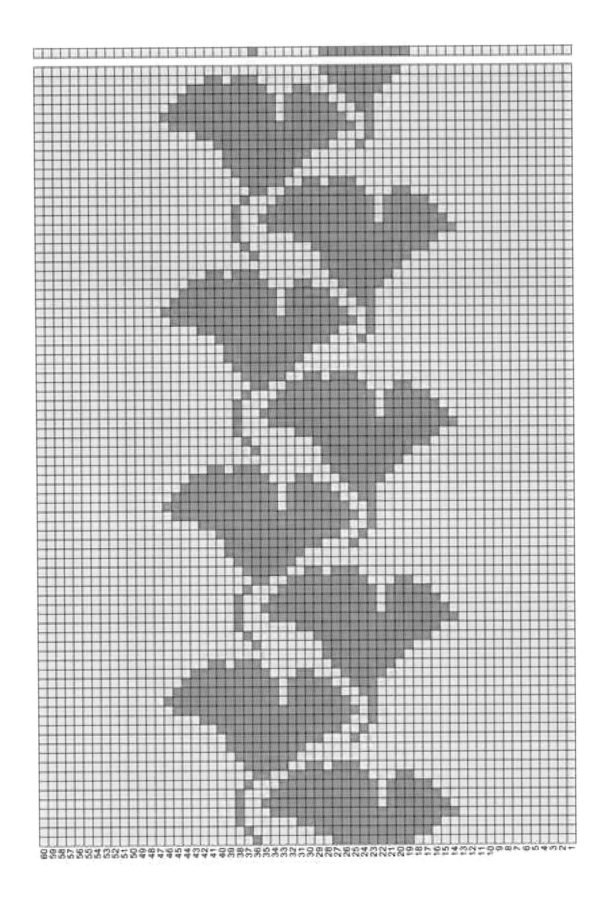

Color as Shape

Knitting a circular piece on circular needles is obvious. You can make sweaters this way—even cardigans with the use of steeks. But, what about something other than a circular tube or a circular shawl? What about a square, a pentagon? Say it with me: "Color can do anything!" In the pattern below, I stranded in the round, employing steeks and five wedges. This produced a cute, cape-like piece that comes together at a point in the front and lies straight across the back. *Saxony* is one of my favorite designs. I love it in the classic colors I originally designed it with, as seen below. I also love it in neutrals, burgundy shades or blues. Change the colors and change the whole mood. This is the perfect shawl for Fall. It is stranded, of course, so there is double wool thickness. It stays put on your shoulders, so there's no need to have hands hold it in place. Whoever thought up steeks is my hero!

Saxony Stranded Open-Front Shawl©

by *Deborah Tomasello*

Courtesy of Solange LaBonne

Size: One Size

Materials: Three 50 g balls of KnitPicks Palette *Jay* (You won't use all of the 3rd ball.)
One 50g ball of each of the following KnitPicks Palatte colors:
Clover
Custard
Canary
Brass Heather
#7 straight needles
One multi-length cable #9 circular needle, five #9 DPNs stitch markers, and tapestry needle
Shawl closure, optional

Abbreviations: M1 = Make a st in st just knitted.
PM = Place marker.

Instructions: Using *Jay*, CO 75 stitches plus 10 steek stitches for a total of 85 stitches. Join to work in the round, taking care not to twist stitches. Begin CHART A on round one: PM, knit 5 steek stitches, knit repeat, PM, repeat chart wedge (5 times total per round), PM between each wedge repeat. End round with 5 more steek stitches. Continue following the chart, beginning and ending each round (**NOT each repeat**) with steek stitches, and increasing as indicated. Knit first steek stitches in the color of the pattern stitch immediately beside it, then alternate colors with colors in that round. Switch to longer cable lengths as needed throughout.

IMPORTANT: Float evenly and loosely every two stitches for a neat-looking shawl back.

NOTE: On round 57, knit 3 sts in center st of each repeat as shown.

After completing round 64, do not knit anymore steek stitches. Disconnect *Clover*. Knit row 65, no longer connecting in the round. Next 9 rows, knit back and forth 2x2 rib in *Jay*. BO loosely.

Cut steeks. Trim edges to 2-3 sts, roll under and stitch to garment.

Neck Edge: Using #7 needles, pick up neck-edge stitches (134 stitches) Knit back and forth, a 2x2 rib for 10 rows. BO loosely.

Finishing: Tie and weave in or trim all color change ends. Wash and block flat, taking care not to stretch out neck edge.

On reading the chart: Please see my YouTube video that explains how to read my colorwork charts and how/where do make the increases: http://www.youtube.com/watch?v=NW7Un1gXRmc

Back view:

CHART A
(next page)

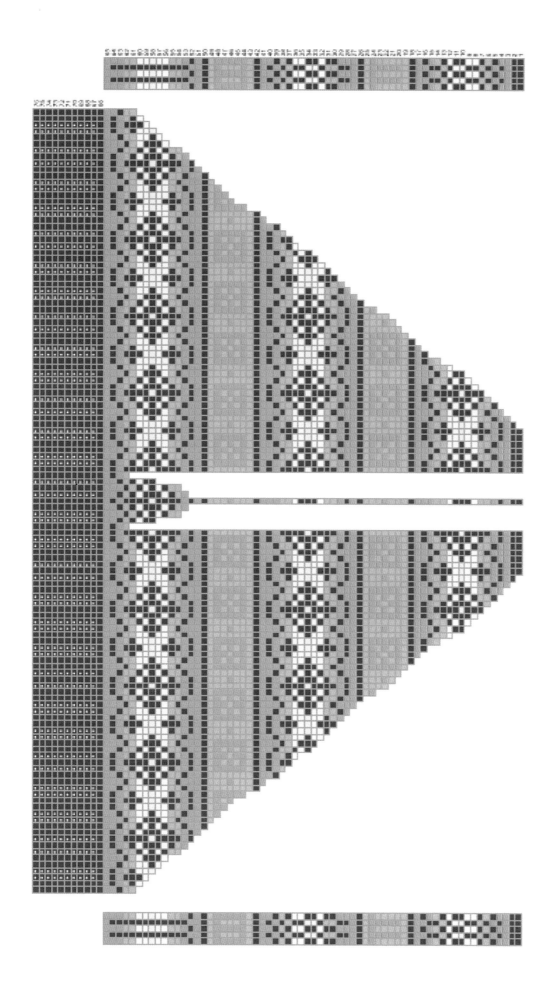

Color as Mood

The fact that color has an effect on mood is well known and has been established repeatedly by numerous scientific studies. In fact, the effect of color on cognitive performance was the topic of my senior thesis in college, and I read more of these studies than I care to remember. (You can find articles relative to mood and color just about everywhere including, *Science Daily* and *Wikipedia* on the Web. Along with purling, I also don't like doing citations. Can you tell?) Some colors invoke anger, some increase positive mood states and enhance job performance. The results are objective rather than subjective. This is to say, certain color-mood connections are seen universally, across age, gender, time and place.

Some colors are calming and others agitate. For my thesis, I replicated a study that hypothesized certain colors used on test paper would predict better results than other colors. Blue paper increased test scores on systematic reasoning tests (those where an answer had to be figured out) compared to the scores from the same test given on red paper. The opposite was true if the exam was a heuristic one (those where the answer sought just popped into the mind. An example: using a number, fill in the blank: ____letters of the alphabet. You just know the answer is 26 without having to give it a lot of calculated reasoning). Scores on this type of test were higher when given on red paper. The results have been replicated, and we know that color does, indeed, affect mood, thinking and more. Because this is so, you can knit mood using color. Amazing, right? When you view the calming cool snowflake shawl, how does it make you feel? Would the same feeling result if you made the shawl using hot pink and orange yarn? Probably not. So, choose your colors and generate a mood. Then cuddle up with this wooly snowflake any way you want! It is a beautiful throw or a warm, comfy wrap. As always, the choice is yours!

SNOWFLAKE STRANDED SHAWL ©

Courtesy of Pia Tomasello

Size: One Size

Materials: Three 50 g balls of KnitPicks Palette *Caribbean*
Two 50 g balls of KnitPicks Palette *White*
One multi-length cable #9 circular needle, five #9 DPNs
Stitch markers and tapestry needle

Abbreviations: M1 = Make a st in st just knitted.
PM = Place marker.

Instructions: 2 DPNs, CO 3 sts using *Caribbean*. K1 row
Purl back for 2nd row.
Add *White*. K1, M1 for 6 sts total
Purl 6 sts
K1, M1 across, starting with *Caribbean* and alternating
with *White*. 6 sts each color for 12 sts total
Purl 12 sts alternating color pattern as previous row.
K1 *Caribbean*, (K1, M1 *White*) for 18 sts total.
Purl 18 sts alternating color pattern as previous row.
K1 *Caribbean*, K1 *White*, (K1, M1 *White*) for 24 sts total.
Split sts evenly on 3 DPNs, 8 sts on each needle, placing
markers every 4 sts. Begin following chart here.
Continue to work in the round. (You will sew opening
closed later.)

IMPORTANT: Float evenly and loosely every two stitches for a neat-looking shawl back.

Follow CHART A beginning with round 1 and adding *White*. Work 6 repeats per round, adding markers between wedges, through round 72. Detach *White*. Knit round 73, then knit the next 4 rounds in a 2x2 rib. BO loosely.

Finishing: Tie and weave in or trim all color change ends. Wash and block flat.

On reading the chart: Please see my YouTube video that explains how to read my colorwork charts and how/where do make the increases: http://www.youtube.com/watch?v=NW7Un1gXRmc

CHART A (next page)

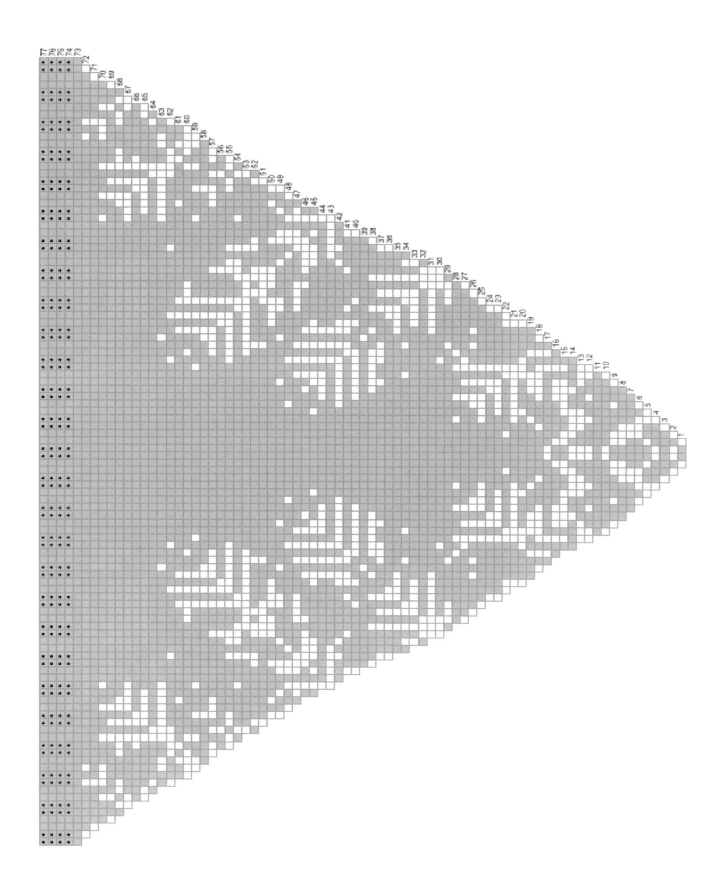

55

Color as Warmth

We don't always knit projects to be worn. Sometimes we just want a warm, cozy lap blanket. Who doesn't? We can knit anything and call it a blanket. But, with *Geometry Rules*, we knit a stranded blanket in the round, making it doubly warm, unique, and stylishly attractive. It's so attractive, in fact, that folded to a triangular shape, it can also be worn as a shawl without looking as though you tossed a blanket over your shoulders. Shhh, don't tell! This is among my favorite designs.

Courtesy of Lauren

Ge☐metry Rules©

by Deborah Tomasello

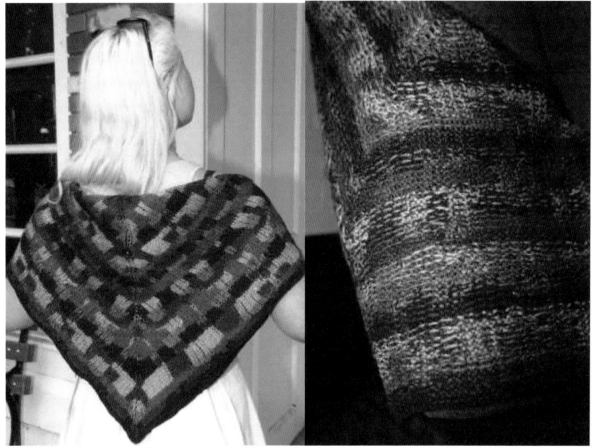

Worn as a shawl: front and backside views Courtesy of Gabby Jacobson

Size: TBD by knitter (at least 44" diameter)

Materials: 2 balls each of KnitPicks Galileo in *Valentine, Black, Sand, Dragonfly,* and *Luminous*
One multi-length cable #10 circular needle, five #10 DPNs, Stitch markers, and tapestry needle

Abbreviations: M1 = Make a st in st just knitted see video:
http://www.youtube.com/watch?v=NW7Un1gXRmc
PM = Place marker.
K2TOG = Knit two stitches together.

Instructions: 2 DPNs, CO 4 sts *Valentine.* K1, M1 for 8 sts total
Purl 8 sts
K1, M1 for 16 sts total
Purl 16 sts
Split sts evenly on 4 DPNs, 4 sts on each needle.
Continue to work in the round
(You will sew opening closed later.)

IMPORTANT: Float evenly and loosely every two stitches for a neat-looking shawl back.

Add *Black* and, beginning with round one, work CHART A as follows: PM, K one chart repeat, PM around (8 chart repeats per round. 8 markers placed.) When you have increased enough sts to warrant it, move work from DPNs to short circular, and switch to longer cable lengths as needed throughout.

After completing round 70, detach *Sand.* With *Black,* knit the next round. Purl round 72. Knit round 73. BO.

Finishing: With tail from CO, sew closed small slit left at the beginning when knitting the first few rounds. Tie and weave in or trim all color change ends. Wash and block flat.

On reading the chart: Please see my YouTube video that explains how to read my colorwork charts and how/where do make the increases: http://www.youtube.com/watch?v=NW7Un1gXRmc

CHART A (next page)

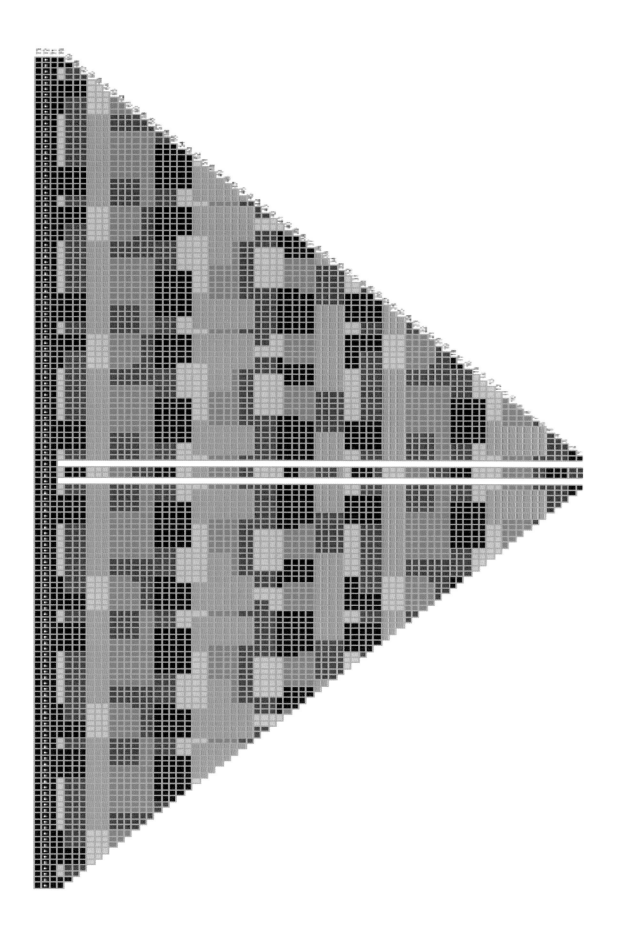

Color as Sunscreen

We all have umbrellas lying around for those miserable, rainy days. How often have you wished for a sunbrella that wouldn't look ridiculous? Carrying a black umbrella to shield us from the strong ultra-violet sun rays feels silly and, well, *wrong*! So, with colorwork, you can create a stunning, lightweight sunbrella that will do the job and look lovely while doing it!

Courtesy of Alexa

WendyP Parasol©

Courtesy of Alexa

Size: TBD by knitter (at least 44" diameter)

Materials: 100 g of KnitPicks Chroma for background color and two
50 g balls of KnitPicks contrasting Palette for main color.
One multi-length cable #9 circular needle, five #9 DPNs,
Stitch markers, and tapestry needle
One umbrella shell, with fabric removed if desired
Needle and thread for attaxching parasol to frame

Abbreviations: M1 = Make a st in st just knitted.

PM = Place marker.

K2TOG = Knit two stitches together.

PSSO= Pass slipped stitch off.

YO = Yarn over.

Instructions: 2 DPNs, CO 4 sts using main color. K1, M1 for 8 sts total
Purl 8 sts
K1, M1 for 16 sts total
Purl 16 sts
K1, (K1, M1) for 24 sts total. Split sts evenly on 4 DPNs,
6 sts on each needle. Continue to work in the
round. (You will sew the opening later.)

IMPORTANT: Float evenly and loosely every two stitches for a neat-looking shawl back.

Add background color and, beginning with round one, work CHART A as follows: PM, K one chart repeat, PM around (8 chart repeats per round. 8 markers placed.) When you have increased enough sts to warrant it, move work from DPNs to short circular, and switch to longer cable lengths as needed throughout.

After completing round 73, detach background color. With main color, complete CHART B (Rounds 74-78 or 80, depending on how many lace rounds desired).

Finishing: With tail from CO, sew closed small slit left at the beginning when knitting the first few rounds, leaving small hole for metal umbrella point. Tie and weave in or trim all color change ends. Wash and block flat, pinning points to form edge points. Using needle and thread, attach and secure piece to umbrella frame so that it stays in place when opened and closed.

On reading the chart: Please see my YouTube video that explains how to read my colorwork charts and how/where do make the increases: http://www.youtube.com/watch?v=NW7Un1gXRmc

CHART A

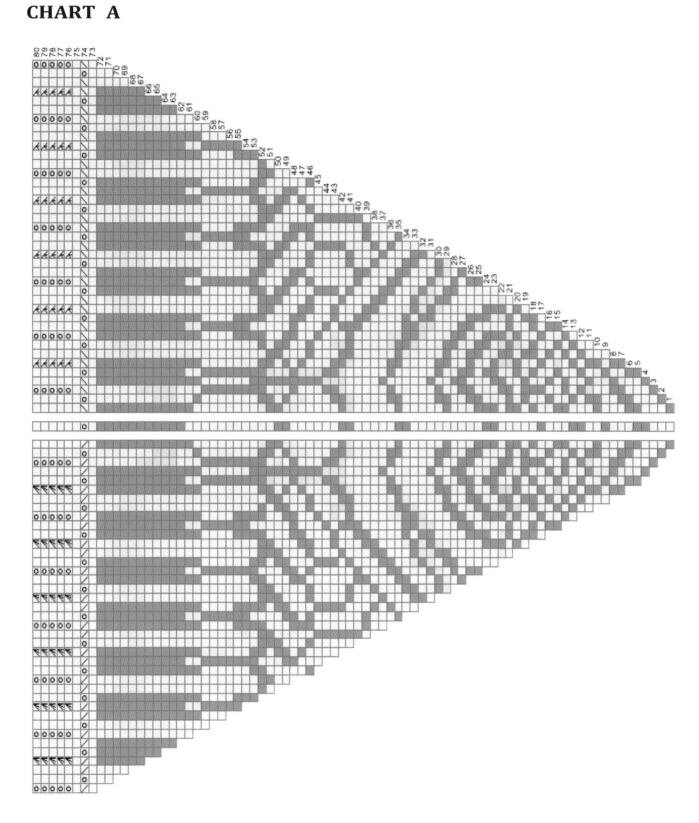

CHART B

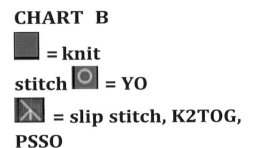

■ = knit
stitch ⊡ = YO
◩ = slip stitch, K2TOG, PSSO

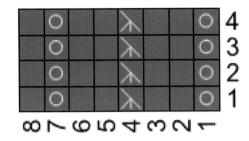

WendyP can also be knitted a little smaller. By working fewer rounds, you can create a shawlette.

Courtesy of Kara (back and front)

If you want a full-sized shawl, you can work more rounds and have that, too!

Courtesy of Alyssa

Color as Color

Remember those colorful cardboard tubes we looked through as kids, watching the shapes inside change as we turned it? For as long as I can remember, I have loved looking through the end of a kaleidoscope. They were (and are) like magic to me. As I turn the cylinder, I watch the colored pebbles fall into place and, as they are reflected over and over by the mirrors inside the tube, wonderfully symmetric and unique designs appear just to please me! Sometimes color is a joy in and of itself. And so it goes with knitted colorwork. Inspired by the kaleidoscope toys of my youth, *Kaleidoscope of Color* is a shawl whose design highlights the wonder of color. Of course, any colors could be substituted for the ones I used, and it would be like a turn of the cylinder. *Voilà!* You've created a brand new pattern to be admired and enjoyed. Knit this full-sized, or stop anywhere along the way for a shawlette. It's always your call. You are the creator of your own piece.

Kaleidoscope of Color
Stranded Shawl©

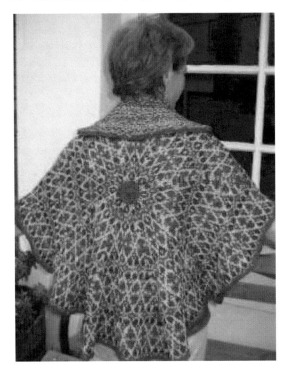

Size: TBD by knitter (at least 45" diameter)

Materials: 3 50 g balls of KnitPicks Palette: *Tomato* (MC)
2 50 g balls of KnitPicks Palette: *Canary*
1 50 g ball each of KnitPicks Palette: *Aurora Heather* and
Calypso Heather plus small amount of *Fairytale*
**Any fingering-weight yarn will do
One multi-length cable #9 circular needle, five #9 DPNs
Stitch markers
Tapestry needle

Abbreviations: M1 = Make a st in st just knitted.
PM = Place marker.
MC = Main color

Instructions: 2 DPNs, CO 4 sts using main color. K1, M1 for 8 sts total
Purl 8 sts
K1, M1 for 16 sts total
Purl 16 sts
K1, (K1, M1) for 24 sts total   Split sts evenly on 4 DPNs,
6 sts on each needle. Continue to work in the
round. (You will sew opening closed later.)

Add *Canary* and, beginning with round one, work CHART A as follows:
PM, K one chart repeat, PM around (8 chart repeats per round. 8
markers placed.) When you have increased enough sts to warrant it,
move work from DPNs to short circular, and switch to longer cable
lengths as needed throughout.
Knit the last 3 rounds as follows: Knit round 74. Purl round 75. BO
round 76, knitwise.

Finishing: With tail from CO, sew closed small slit left at the
beginning when knitting the first few rounds. Tie and weave in or trim
all color change ends. Wash and block flat.

IMPORTANT: Float evenly and loosely every two stitches for a neat-
looking shawl back.

NOTE: On round 57, knit 3 sts in center st (and add marker) of each wedge repeat as shown by green st. 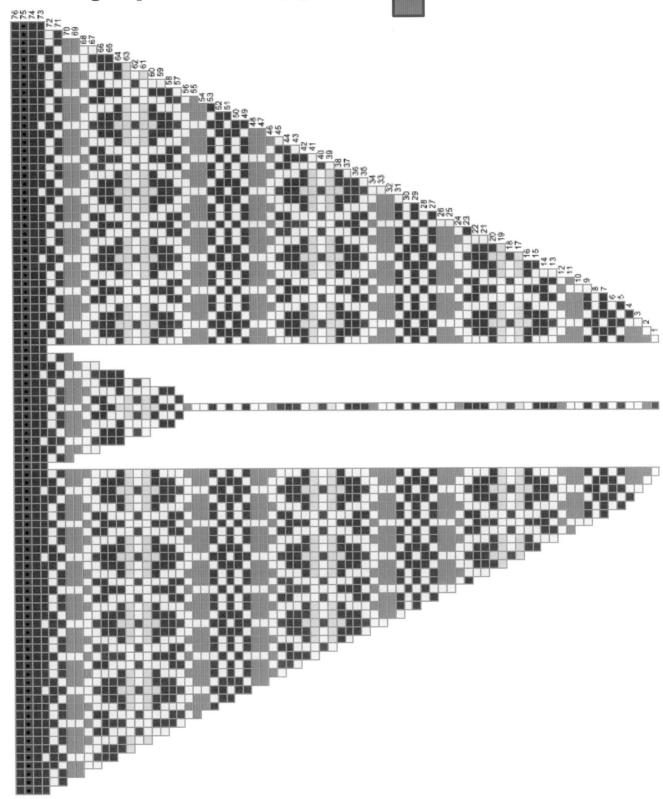 **CHART   A:**

Color as Love

Is there anything sweeter than a brand new baby? When we see a sleeping infant all cuddled up in a handmade blanket, we feel love. We can create the feeling ourselves by making a colorwork baby wrap. Worked in the round like the others, this piece is lined in fleece for warmth as well as to prevent tiny fingers and toes from getting caught in the stranded floats. Use the colors shown in the pattern, or change them up to suit your personal taste. Anyway you knit this blanket, you knit love.

Sweet He♥rts Baby Wrap©

Size: Approx. 36" in diameter

Materials: 2 balls of KnitPicks Palette *White*
1 ball of KnitPicks Palette *Whirlpool*
1 ball of KnitPicka Palette *Hyacinth*
1 ball of KnitPicks Palette *Pistachio*
**Any fingering-weight yarn will do
One multi-length cable #9 circular needle, five #9 DPNs,
stitch markers, and tapestry needle
1.5 yds of white fleece for backing, if desired

Abbreviations: M1 = Make a st in st just knitted.
PM = Place marker.
K2TOG = Knit two stitches together.

Instructions: 2 DPNs, CO 4 sts using *White*. K1, M1 for 8 sts total.
Purl 8 sts.
K1, M1 for 16 sts total.

Purl 16 sts.
K1, (K1, M1) for 24 sts total   Split sts evenly on 4 DPNs,
6 sts on each needle. Continue to work in the round.
(You will sew opening closed later.)

IMPORTANT: Float evenly and loosely every two stitches for a neat-looking shawl back.

Add *Whirlpool* and *Hyacinth* and, beginning with round one, work CHART A as follows: PM, K one chart repeat, PM around (8 chart repeats per round. 8 markers placed.) When you have increased enough sts to warrant it, move work from DPNs to short circular, and switch to longer cable lengths as needed throughout.
After completing round 72, detach all yarns except *White*. With *White*, knit the next round. Knit round 74 as follows: YO, K2TOG around. Knit next 2 rounds. BO.

Finishing: With tail from CO, sew closed small slit left at the beginning when knitting the first few rounds. Tie and weave in or trim all color change ends. Wash and block flat.

Cut fleece to fit back of blanket so that, when the last 2 knit rows are folded back, they create a picot edge and cover the fleece edge. Hand - stitch knitting to fleece.

On reading the chart: Please see my YouTube video that explains how to read my colorwork charts and how/where do make the increases: http://www.youtube.com/watch?v=NW7Un1gXRmc

CHART A

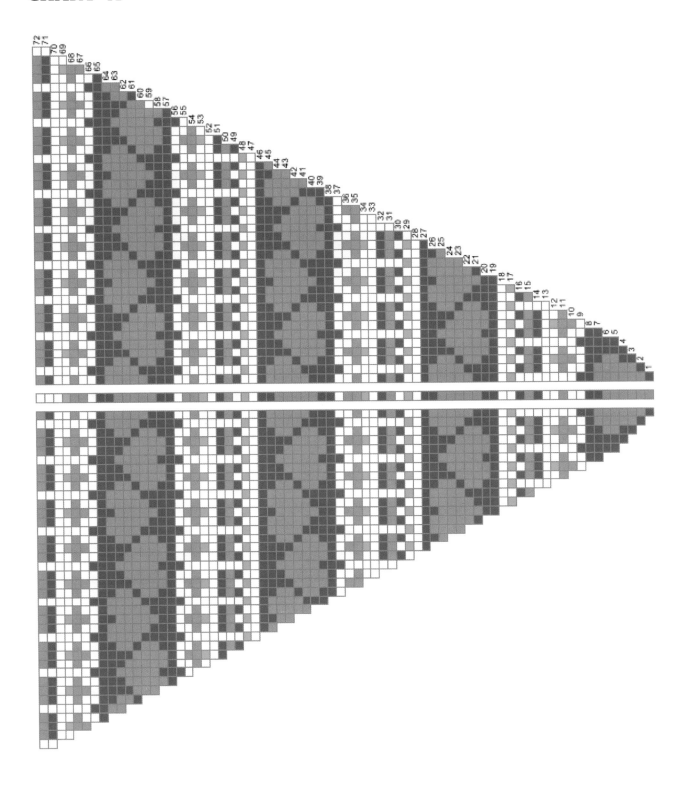

Color Combination Knitting

Sometimes it's fun to mix things up a little. Who says you must knit a project all in a single style, stitch, color scheme or even yarn weight? You can mix and match (or not) to your heart's content. Maybe you were told that blue, gray and brown shouldn't be put together. Or maybe green and orange with a red or rose? Why not? If you like it, it goes. It's fun to experiment with combining yarn weights, too. Adding a bulky weight yarn to a piece primarily worked with fingering weight yarn adds interest and alleviates any monotony that might be inherent in a design. I decided, after knitting about a dozen colorwork shawls, that it might be fun to add a simple lace stitch motif to break up the colorwork design. *Blue Diamonds* (cover pattern modeled by my gorgeous friend, Stacy) is the result. It is no more difficult to work than straight-forward colorwork, and it adds interest to the shawl. This opens doors to virtually endless design possibilities. So exciting!

Blue Diamonds: Color and Lace

Stranded Shawl©

Cover design model: Stacy DeYoung

Size: TBD by knitter (at least 45" diameter)

Materials: 1 100 g skein of Lisa Souza Hardtwist Petite: *Sapphire*
1 100 g skein of Lisa Souza Hardtwist Petite: *Turqua*
1 100 g skein of Lisa Souza Hardtwist Petite: *Bluegrass*
1 100 g skein of Lisa Souza Hardtwist Petite: *Seafoam*
One multi-length cable #9 circular needle, five #9 DPNs
Stitch markers
Tapestry needle

Abbreviations: M1 = Make a st in st just knitted.
PM = Place marker.
K2Tog = Knit two stitches together.
YO = Yarn over.

Instructions: Using 2 PDPNs, and leaving long tail, CO 4 sts using *Turqua*.
K1, M1 for 8 sts total.
Purl 8 sts.
K1, M1 for 16 sts total.
Purl 16 sts.
K1, (K1, M1) for 24 sts total   Split sts evenly on 4 DPNs, 6 sts on each needle. Continue to work in the round.   (You will sew opening closed later.)

IMPORTANT: Float evenly and loosely every two stitches for a neat-looking shawl back.

Add *Sapphire* and, beginning with round one, work CHART A through round 43 as follows: PM, K one chart repeat, PM around (8 chart repeats per round. 8 markers placed.) When you have increased enough sts to warrant it, move work from DPNs to short circular, and switch to longer cable lengths as needed throughout.
Round 44—YO, K2Tog to last sts of each repeat, k1.
Round 45—YO, K2Tog around.

Round 46—YO, K2Tog to center st (24 sts), PM, K1, YO, K2Tog to last st, K1—51 sts in each of 8 sections.

Round 47–K.

Rounds 48-57, work CHART A.

Round 58—YO, K2Tog to last sts of each repeat, K1.

Round 59—YO, K2Tog around.

Round 60—YO, K2Tog to center st (30 sts), K center st, YO, K2Tog to last st, K—63 sts in each of 8 sections.

Round 61—K according to chart, M1,K1,M1 in center stitch as indicated. (65 sts in each section)

NOTE: Because of increases, center stitch will shift left. Move marker as needed so it is placed directly before the center stitch.

Rounds 62-78, Work CHART A.

Round 79—YO, K2Tog to last st of each section, K. Remove all but first marker as you go.

Rounds 80 and 81—YO, K2Tog around.

Round 82—K.

Round 83—BO.

Finishing: With tail from CO, sew closed small slit left at the beginning when knitting the first few rounds. Tie and weave in or trim all color change ends. Wash and block flat.

NOTE: On round 61, knit 3 sts in center st (moving and replacing marker) of each repeat as shown.

CHART A

Center square on round 43: place marker.

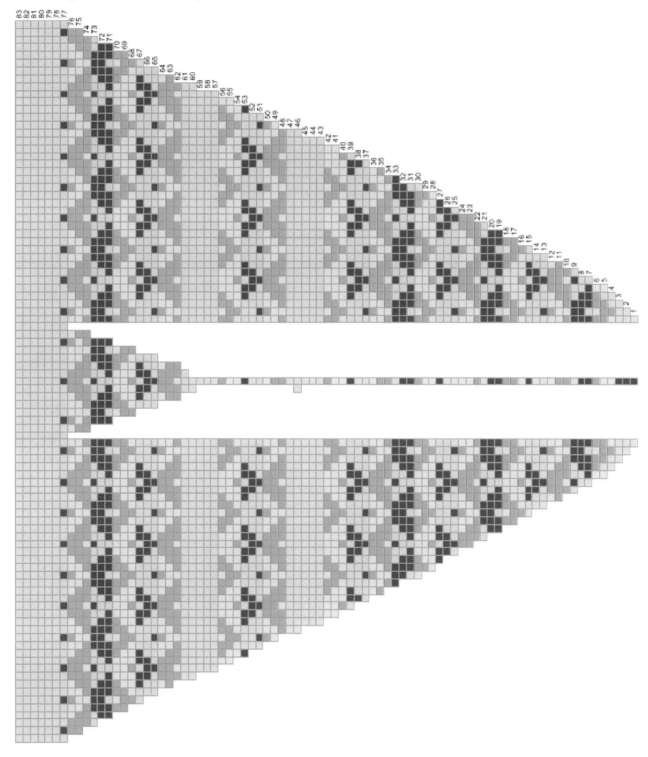

About Deborah Tomasello

"Some people see a gorgeous sunset and photograph it. Others paint it. I knit it. Fiber and fabric are my media. Knitting the sunset makes it mine."

Deborah Tomasello learned to knit and sew at her grandmother's knee when she was about five years old. Some of her fondest memories of her Gramma involve yarn and needles. She would start with grand ideas of knitting a scarf, but after working a few inches, when something of a lacy trapezoid would appear, she'd turn that scarf-gone-awry into a skirt for her Barbie. Over the years, her scarves became straighter, and her imagination broadened. Wools and fabrics have woven themselves into Deborah's very being, and she spends all her days happily designing and knitting her colorwork patterns.

Contact Info

Deborah Tomasello
CoeDeborah@aol.com
http://www.ravelry.com/groups/colorworksbydebi-deborah-tomasello-designs

Video Tutorials

http://www.youtube.com/watch?v=c7JJc9-_eO0
http://www.youtube.com/watch?v=8N5udL05kAo
http://www.youtube.com/watch?v=NW7Un1gXRmc

Made in the USA
Charleston, SC
04 January 2014